This book was first published in 1990 by Princess House
an imprint of Studio Editions Ltd
Princess House, 50 Eastcastle Street
London W1N 7AP, England

World Copyright, Text & Illustrations © Princess House, 1990

Text written by Jacqueline Fortey

ISBN 1 85170 337 3

Printed and bound Hungary

CHESTER THE MOUSE
OPPOSITES BOOK

ILLUSTRATED BY JANE HARVEY

Chester finds a huge mouse
Which gives him a clue
To a special new game
That you can play too.
There are word pairs to find
And as you will see,
The words must be different
As different can be.
The toy mouse is *Large*
While Chester is *Small*,
But Chester's quite *Short*
And toy mouse is *Tall* . . .
Now you've learnt how it works
Are you ready to go
Hunting opposite words?
Looking high, looking low!

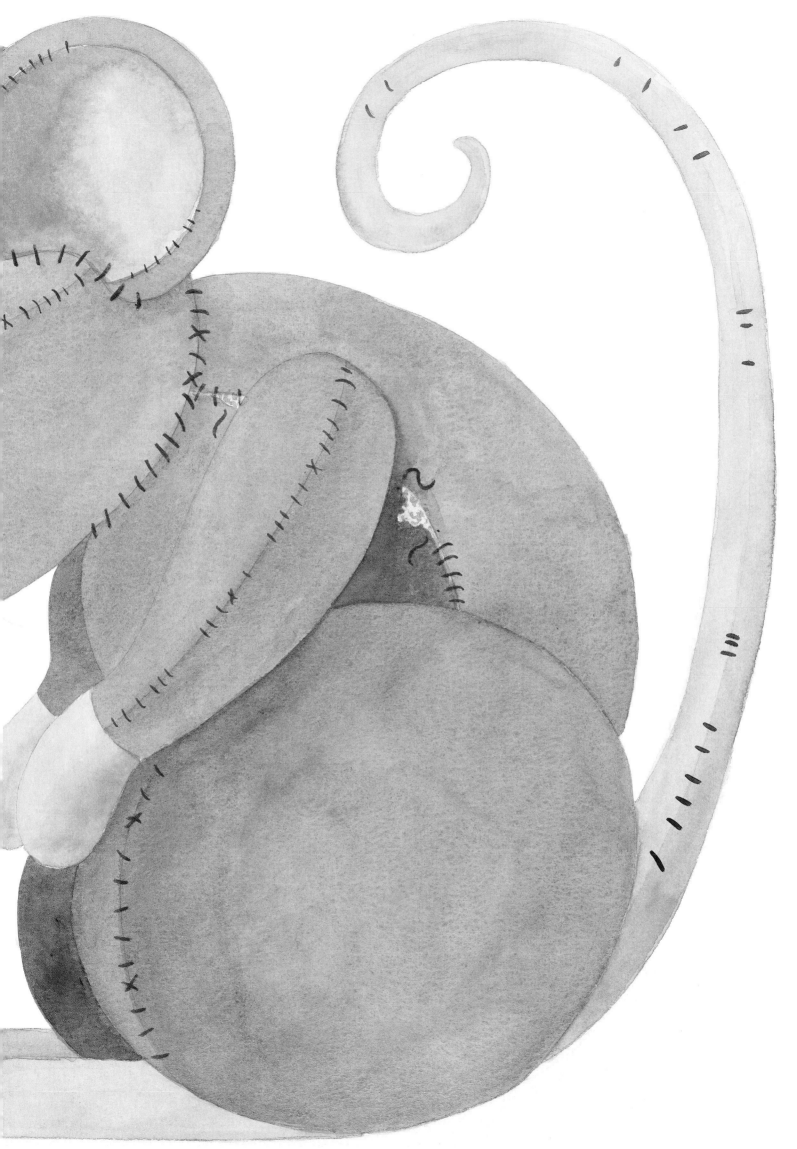

In
Out

Max is in, Chester's out,
They've already begun!
And our opposites game
Is going to be fun.

Fat
Thin

Here are two jolly men
Each with a wide grin,
Their clothes are the same,
But one's fat and one's thin.

Noisy
Quiet

There's no more peace now!
With a Rum-tum-ti-tum,
Noisy Chester walks by
Banging hard on his drum.

Hot
Cold

Now which drink will he try?
The glass is ice cold,
But the steaming teacup
Is too hot to hold.

Old New

Now here are two old shoes
All tattered and torn,
And here are two new ones –
They've never been worn.

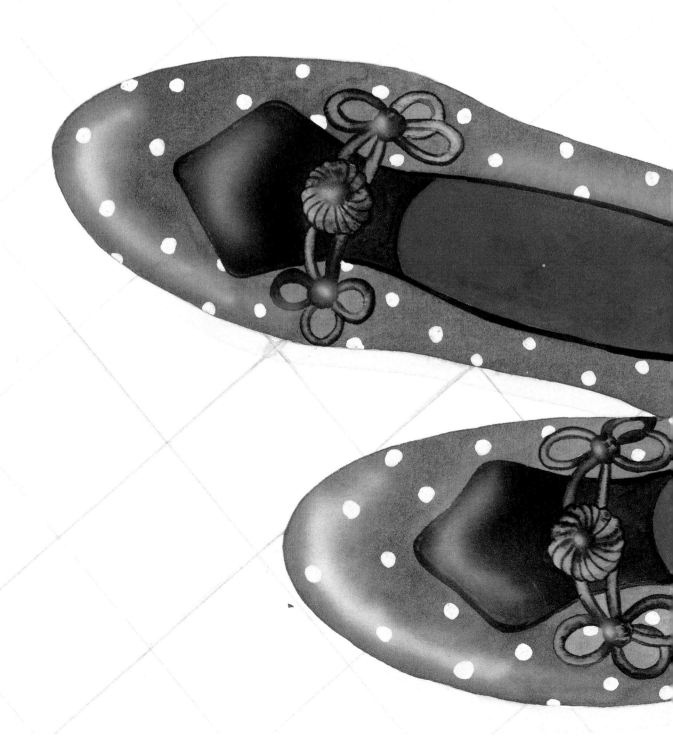

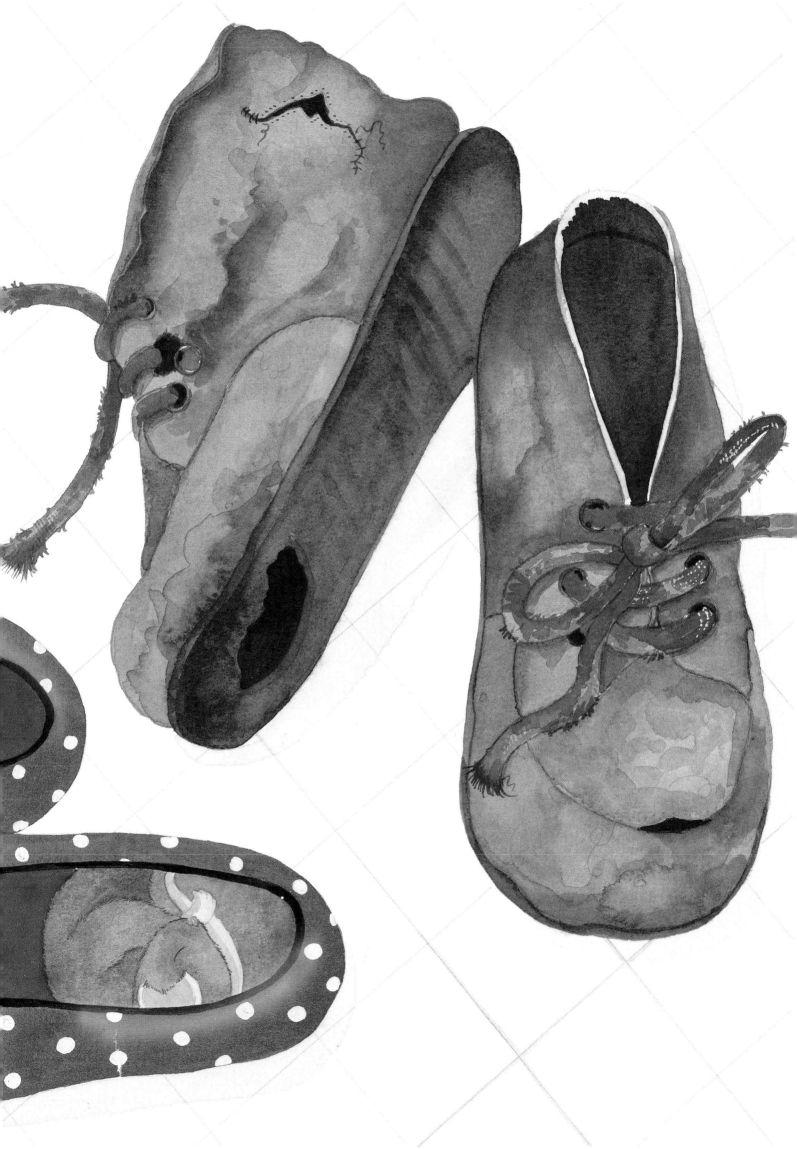

Sunny
Cloudy

The weather house lady
Pops out in the sun,
But the weather man thinks
That the clouds are more fun.

Awake
Asleep

Who's snuggled up here?
Chester climbs up to peep.
There's kangaroo's baby
Curled up fast asleep.

Fierce
Timid

Fierce lions, it's said
Are nervous of mice,
But this mouse runs off
Without looking twice!

Sad
Happy

Now these bouncy balloons
Have just had a race.
Which one came first –
Can you tell by its face?

Up
Down

Chester soars up so high
On a see-saw he's found,
That his friend elephant
Sinks right down to the ground.

On Off

There is not enough room
For two Teds on this chair,
And the one tumbling off
Is a very cross bear.

Tall Short

Now these five soldier dolls
Share a look of surprise.
Four are tall, one is short:
Chester measures his size.

Wrapped Unwrapped

Chester unwrapped a gift,
What a lovely surprise!
And who's that wrapped up,
Can you just see his eyes?

Open
Closed

One box lid flies open,
Jack jumps up with glee.
The other one's closed
So there's no-one to see.

Front
Back

These two wobbly puppets
Who dance too and fro,
First face front, then face back,
In Chester's new show.

Full
Empty

Max grasps his jar tight
As it's full to the brim,
But poor Chester's is empty
No candy for him!

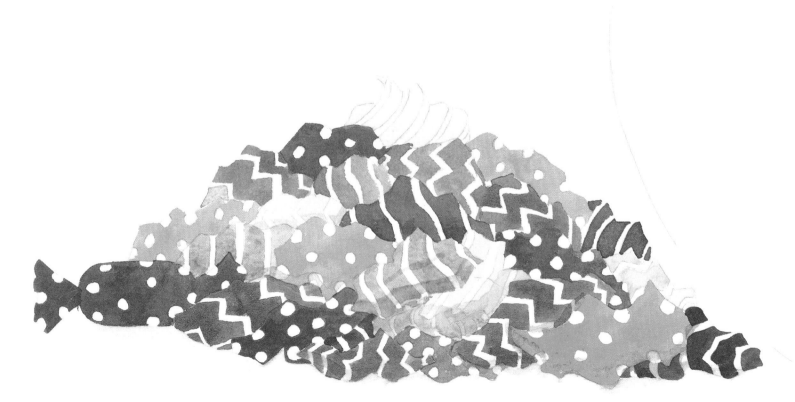

Black White

Chester the artist
Has painted two mice,
A black one, a white one,
They both look so nice.

Hard Soft

A choice of two chairs
For our mouse's short rest.
One is hard, one is soft –
Which does Chester like best?

Fast
Slow

Just testing for speed,
On your marks, get set, go!
No prizes for guessing
Who's fast and who's slow.

Before
After

The toys before painting
Are not very bright,
But after they're finished
The colours look right.

Light Dark

Chester holds up a torch
With a bright beam of light.
It can help him to see
On this very dark night.

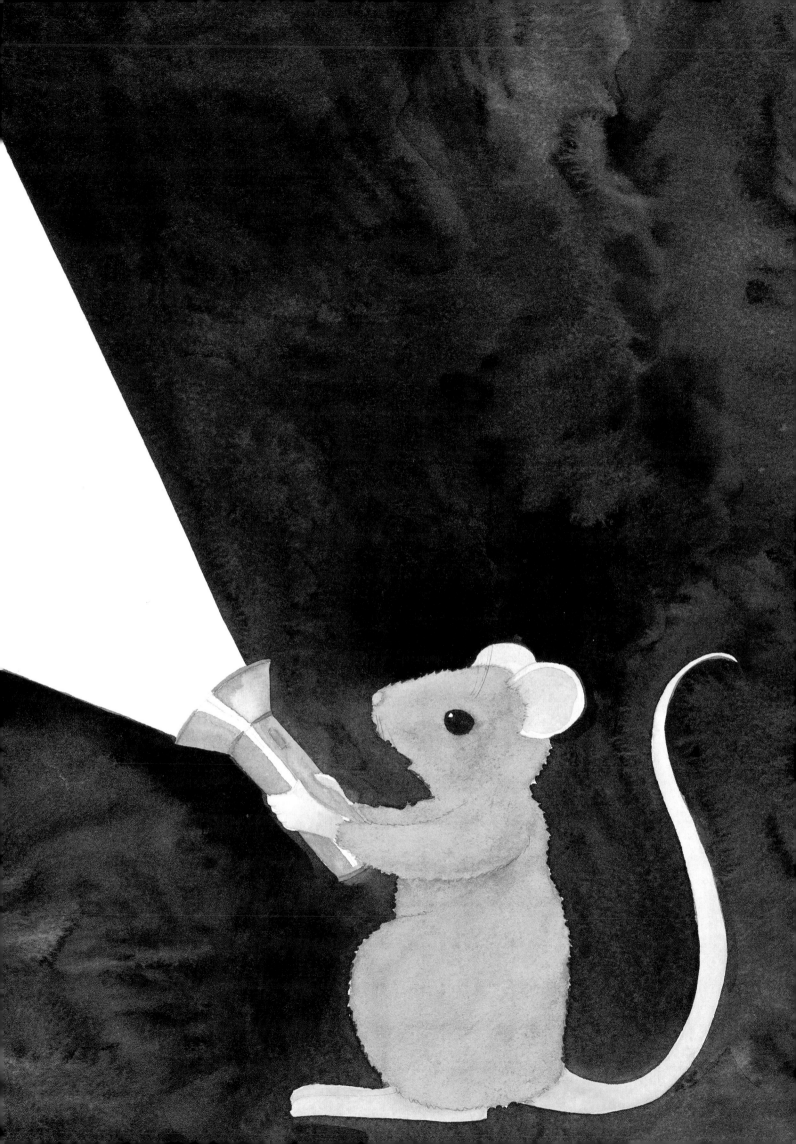

Shaky
Steady

That tower looks shaky,
It could topple and fall.
Do you think it could crush
Chester's nice, steady wall?

Broken
Fixed

The horses are broken
And looking so sad.
When Chester has fixed them
Oh, won't they be glad!

Heavy
Light

The light dainty mouse
Rises high on the scale,
But our heavy mouse lands
With a bump, on his tail.

Big
Little

Mother elephant's so big,
Squeezed tight in her place.
Little baby curls up in
A much smaller space.

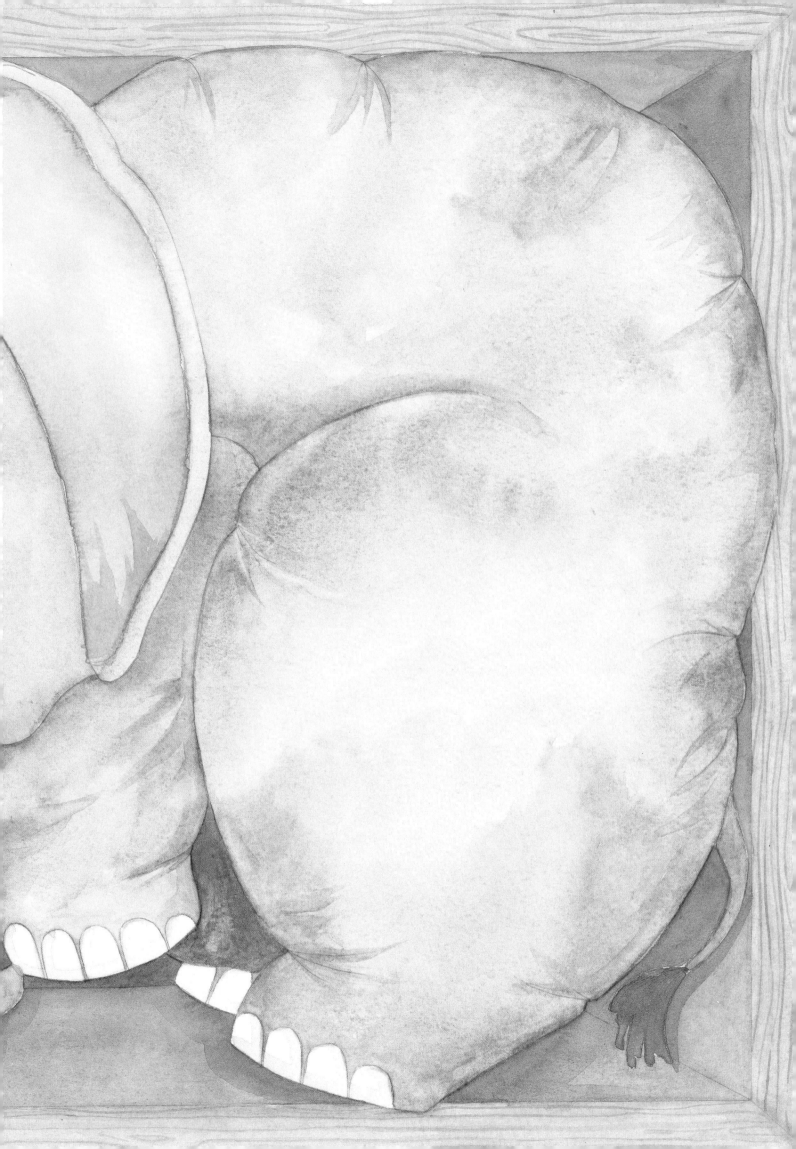

Push
Pull

Who's working harder
The cat or the mouse?
As one pushes, one pulls
A train round the house.

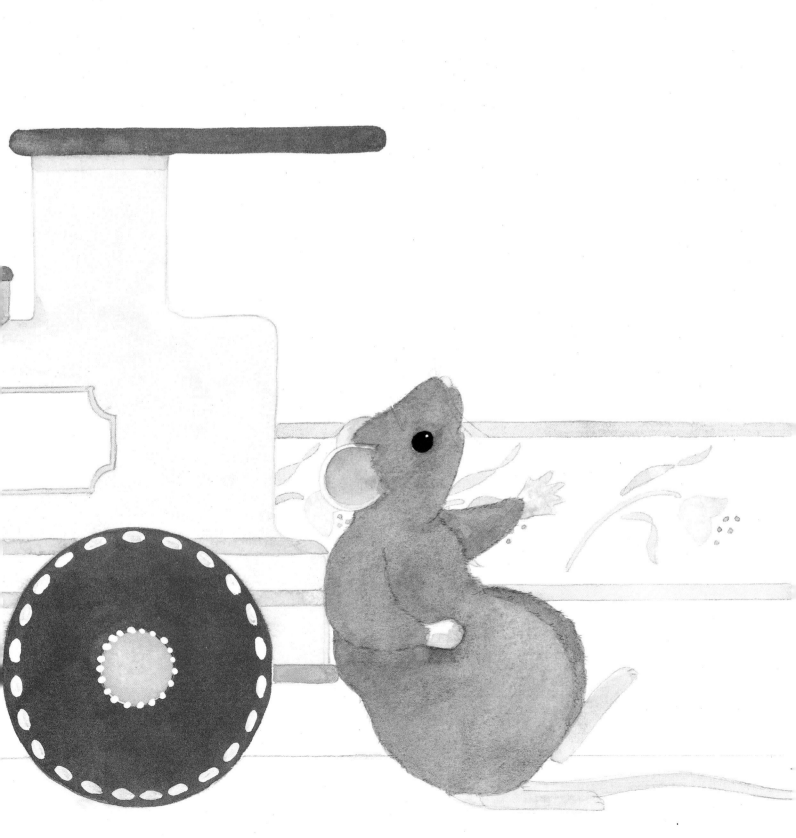

Chester meets up with
A tiny mouse friend
Who's missed the beginning
But is here for the end.
Now help him match pairs
Of the words you have found –
They are all on this page,
You can guide him around.

Front

Soft

Black

Wrapped

Little

Light

Dark

Broken

Out

Thin

Shaky

Slow

In

Noisy

Fat

White

Timid

Light

Fixed

Steady

Sad

Open

Cold

On

H

nwrapped

Tall

Big

Short

Full

Sunny

Cloudy

Back

Hard

Quiet

Asleep

Fierce

Off

Up

ot

Empty

Awake

Happy

fter

Before

Down

Push

Fast

Full

Closed

Old